MARVEL STUDIOS

SPIDER-MAN

No Way Home

MUSIC FROM THE MOTION PICTURE SOUNDTRACK

Music by Michael Giacchino

ISBN 978-1-70516-226-2

Visit Hal Leonard Online at
www.halleonard.com

Contact us:
Hal Leonard
7777 West Bluemound Road
Milwaukee, WI 53213
Email: info@halleonard.com

In Europe, contact:
Hal Leonard Europe Limited
42 Wigmore Street
Marylebone, London, W1U 2RN
Email: info@halleonardeurope.com

In Australia, contact:
Hal Leonard Australia Pty. Ltd.
4 Lentara Court
Cheltenham, Victoria, 3192 Australia
Email: info@halleonard.com.au

CONTENTS

DAMAGE CONTROL

Written by
MICHAEL G. GIACCHINO

Moderately fast

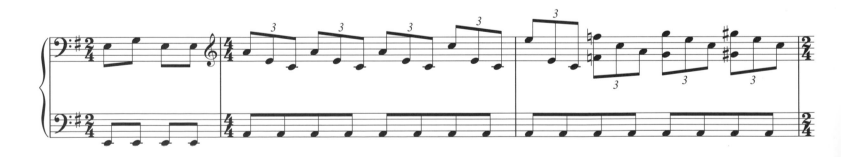

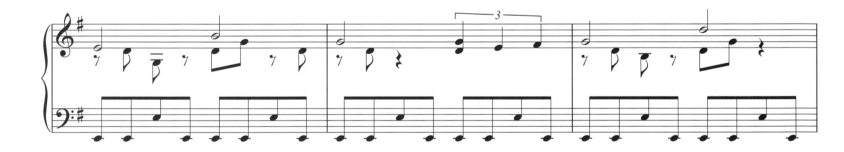

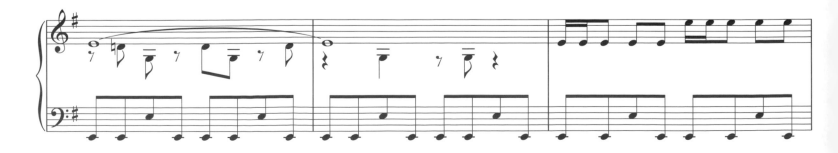

BEING A SPIDER BITES

Written by
MICHAEL G. GIACCHINO

OTTO TROUBLE

Written by MICHAEL G. GIACCHINO
and DANNY ELFMAN

Moderately slow

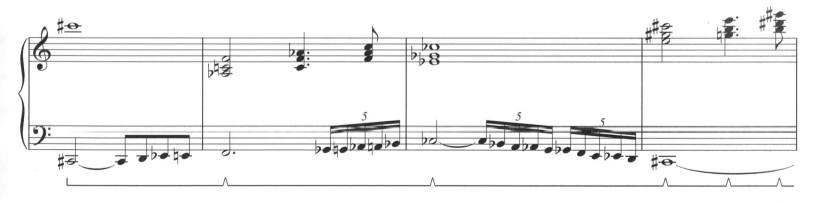

Moderately fast

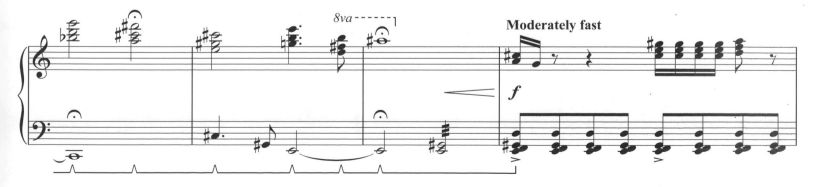

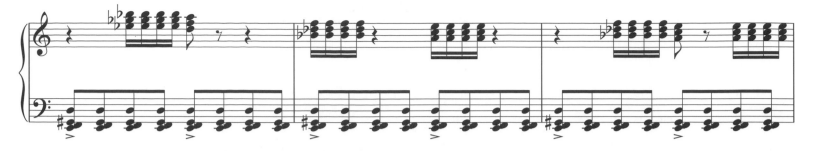

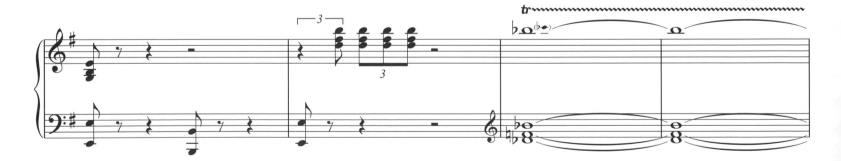

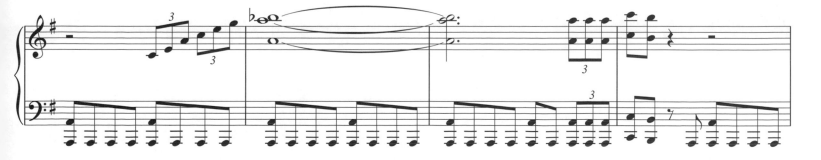

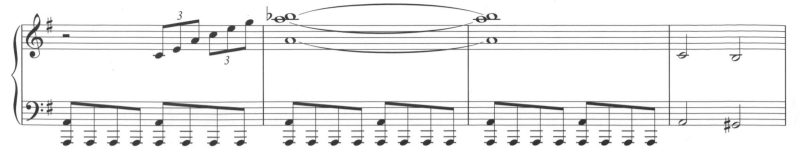

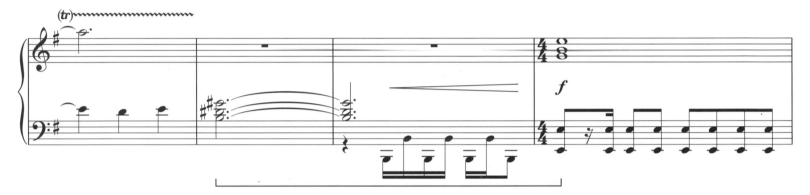

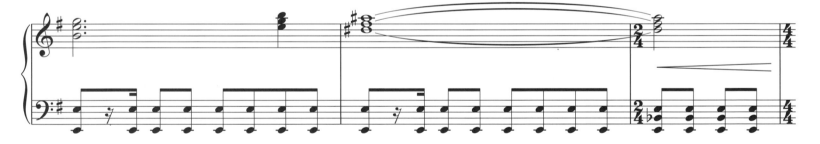

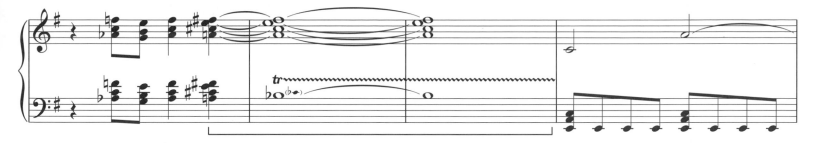

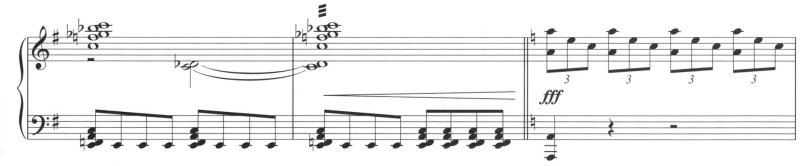

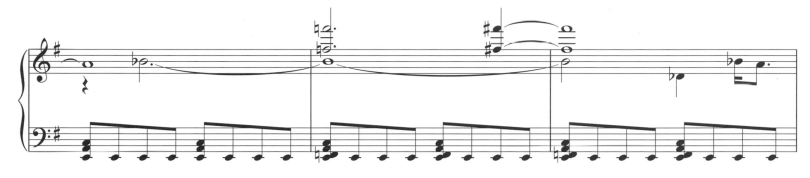

ALL SPELL BREAKS LOOSE

Written by
MICHAEL G. GIACCHINO

Moderately

Pedal ad lib. throughout

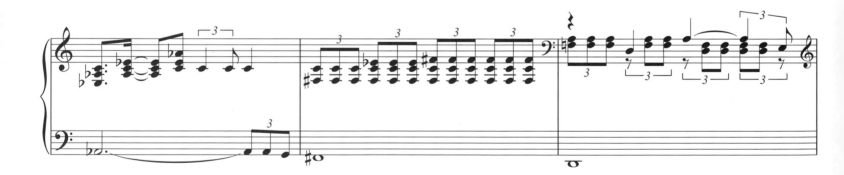

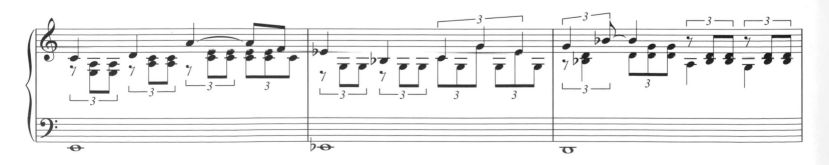

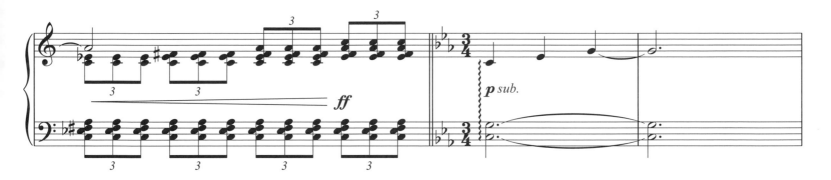

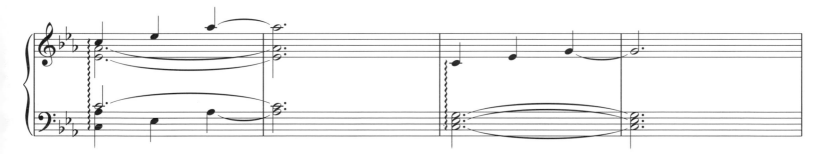

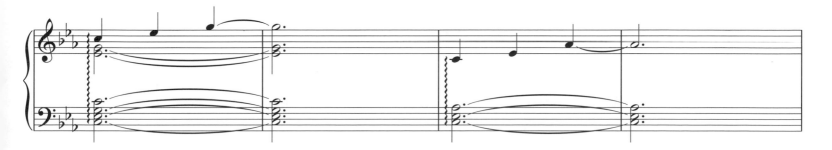

Slightly Faster

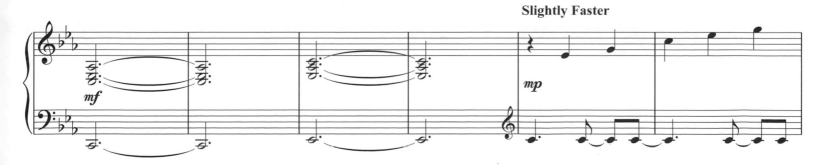

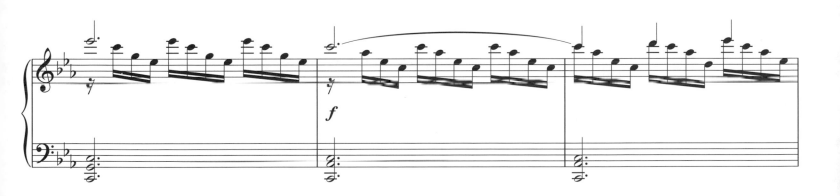

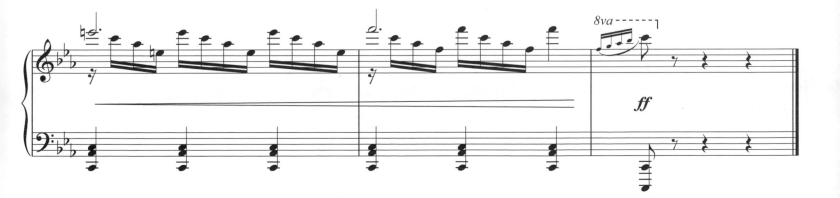

EXIT THROUGH THE LOBBY

Written by
MICHAEL G. GIACCHINO

Slowly

Pedal ad lib. throughout

A DOOM WITH A VIEW

Written by
MICHAEL G. GIACCHINO

Moderately, not too fast

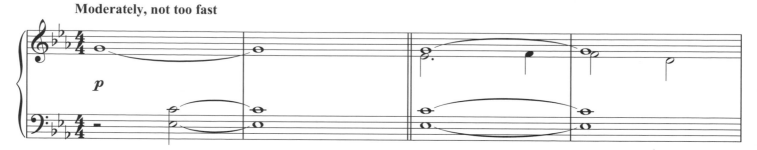

Moderately slow

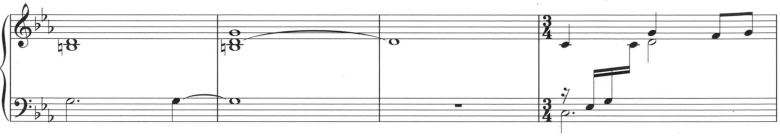

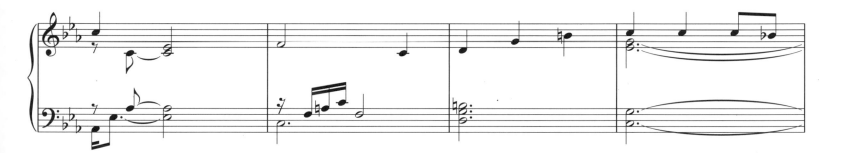

rit.

SPIDER BAITING

Written by
MICHAEL G. GIACCHINO

Moderately slow

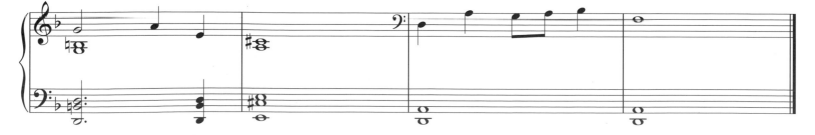

LIBERTY PARLANCE

Written by
MICHAEL G. GIACCHINO

Moderately fast

Slowly, forcefully

MONSTER SMASH

Written by
MICHAEL G. GIACCHINO

Moderately fast, in 2

SHIELD OF PAIN

Written by MICHAEL G. GIACCHINO,
JAMES HORNER and DANNY ELFMAN

Moderately slow, expressively

Pedal ad lib. throughout

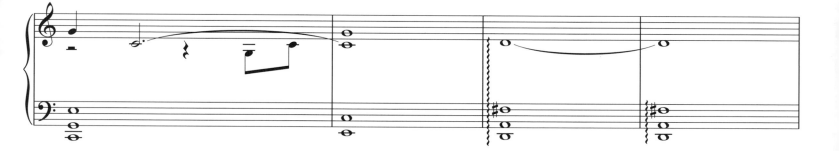

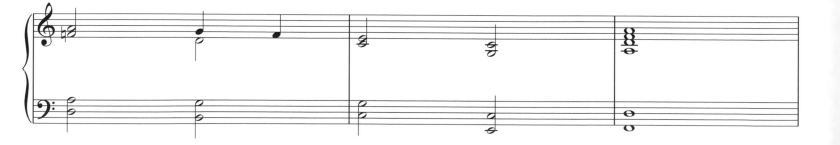

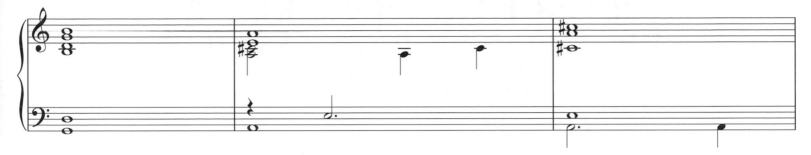

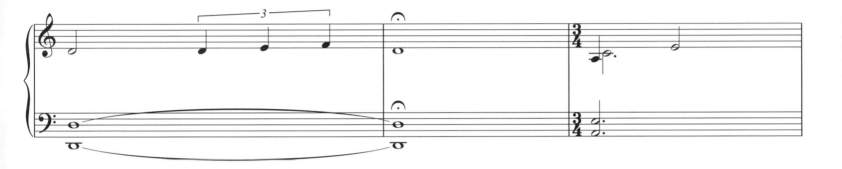

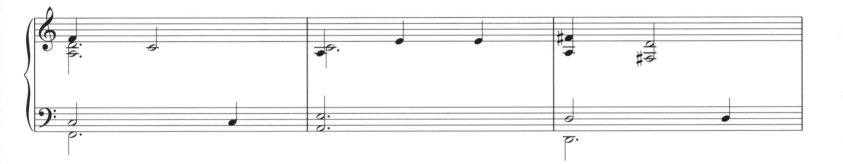

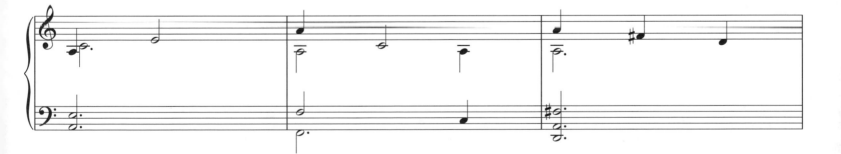

PETER PARKER PICKED A PERILOUSLY PRECARIOUS PROFESSION

Written by
MICHAEL G. GIACCHINO

cresc. poco a poco

accel.

Moderately

f

molto rall.

ff

SPIDER-MAN: NO WAY HOME MAIN THEME

Written by
MICHAEL G. GIACCHINO

Moderately

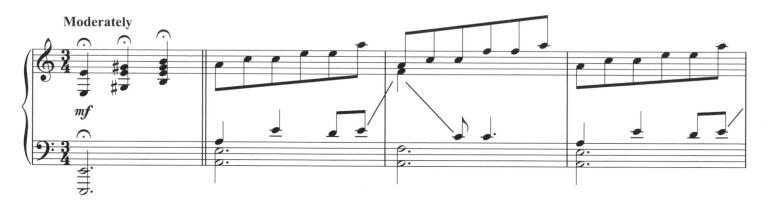

Moderately fast

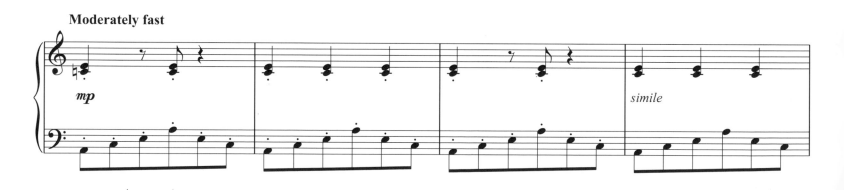

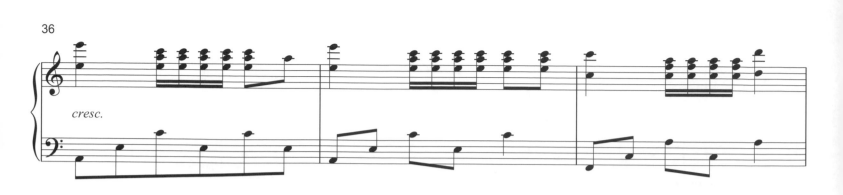

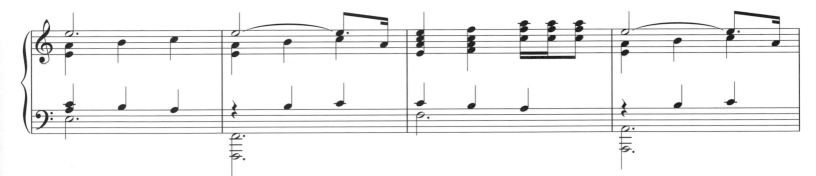

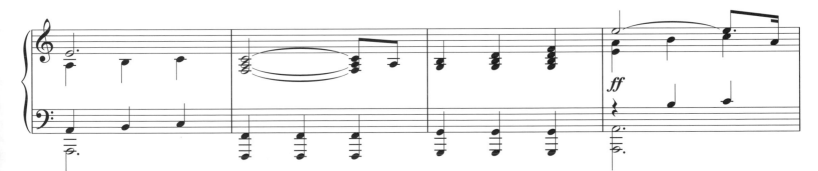

FORGET ME KNOTS

Written by
MICHAEL G. GIACCHINO

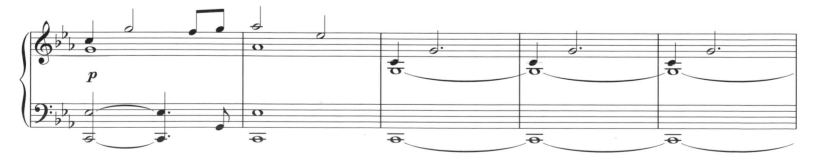

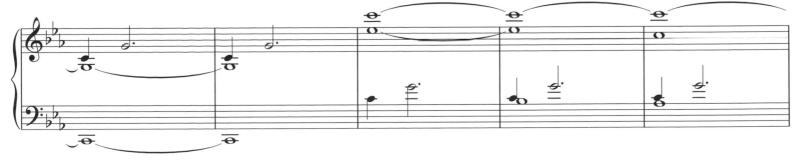

Slower

accel.

Tempo I

f

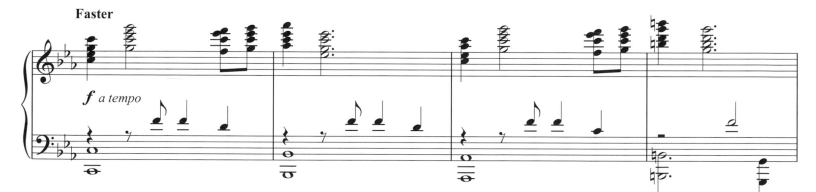